Mercury HeartLink
www.heartlink.com

Here There
is Also
Burning

Here There
is Also
Burning

Stewart S. Warren

Here There is Also Burning
Copyright ©2012 Stewart S. Warren

ISBN: 978-0-9854153-0-3
Publisher: Mercury HeartLink
Printed in the United States of America

Front cover photograph by **Andrea Byrnes**, *www.egyptological.com*

Back cover photograph and on page 154 by **Dee Cohen**

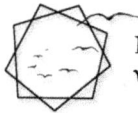

Mercury HeartLink
www.heartlink.com

Contents

SOMEONE SWEET
SHOWED ME THIS DIRT

A BELL HAS FOUND US

PROBE UNTIL A POOL APPEARS

PALMS UP
WITH A BLINDFOLD ON

FOREWORD

Here There is Also Burning is Stewart S. Warren's tenth full-length collection of poetry. Whatever your poetic tastes, core beliefs or temperament, you will not be able to read this book complacently. You will engage it emotionally, intellectually, spiritually or, more likely, in some combination thereof. *Here There is Also Burning* is a fusion of dearly held and deeply ingrained American character, folklore and myth. Warren doesn't simply talk about these things: his poetry embodies them. He has listened long and patiently to this land and its people, and his voice is, like Walt Whitman's and Woody Guthrie's, a genuine and compelling vernacular whorl, a transformative narration and description of the Southwest that goes cosmic.

As the biographical sketch at book's end makes clear, Stewart Warren "holds no university degrees." Neither is his poetry academic. However, this collection is, in both its poetics and imaginative vision, part of a watershed in and of American poetry. It answers the challenge that Wallace Stevens set for his own and American poetry in the mid Twentieth Century: Poetry must teach us "how to live and what to do." These poems do that, without preaching, in a powerful music and drumbeat that arises partly from the author's many years as a percussionist and wholly from his heart. The poet and his poems beautifully, believably and optimistically render his and our lives into free verse. Stewart Warren is an itinerate on the road to the sacred.

Gregory L. Candela
Professor Emeritus, University of New Mexico

for the community of poets
in Alburquerque, New Mexico

for those who speak truth to power
through their gift of vision and voice

for the voiceless

A Santo Niño Candle
Flickers Until Dawn

Day After the Rain

It was not the electric dust
and frenzy of ions, nor
the sharp tang of lightning in the nose.
It was not the crushing wave
that rolls ahead of the storm,
    not the tall walking rain.
It was the day after.

Hills at the edge of the desert
    know gratitude
like the last sibling in line.
There were fingers deep in the soil;
there were tiny lakes in the cracks
and drops in the curves of leaves.
It was everything resumed.

Shorter green wings
that had paused in the drought
    began to leaf,
continue in their quest.
Life rose as smells, circus acts,
fragrances in every range.
A praying mantis perched on a twig.

This is the wafer put in the mouth.
This is the dew between her legs.
This is some kind of heaven or
    a path down to the sea.
Needlessly, you plead the word *reprieve*
as if you'd been forgotten.

OVERCAST

Grey is not a good enough word.
But after being raised
on Light Emitting Diodes and ™Disney

what would I know of nuance?
November's another meaning.
You've got to start

all over again
to find the faces in this scene.
The art of black and white

is also overdone.
I was never taught to see
the blue in brown,

the shades of temperature
in one small gust of wind.
That which turns us

toward darkness brings us
back to the light. Sometimes
I get more work done in shadow.

WATER FOR CHRISTMAS
the card from WaterAid America

Left to right it's peace on earth,
repeating lady bug patterns,
a snowy farm scene
in dark green pointillism—
Christmas cards like wings
open in a row.

In rural New Mexico a mother
pulls bread from an *orno*
on a wooden paddle, her children
looking doe-eyed into
the brush of the painter,
some sheep, crows, winter sun.

This is how it goes
in folded cards
across my bookshelf. Oh,
and one more, an African girl
in black and white—except
for the bright blue plastic pan
of clear water on her head.

Below the equator
my other mouth smiles.

2ᴺᴰ DAY OF SPRING
February 4ᵗʰ 2012

We're all here, everyone
who's supposed to be.
I can't laugh about it all the time
but I'm on the brink
of something behind the pain.

I've been working this corner
for longer than I care to remember;
one by one the indictments
then the acquittals. It's too slow,
and they just keep coming.

And people ask if I have a job—
are you kidding?
The project is *innocence*,
but no one can tell me for sure
if there's a deadline.

I'd like to shortcut the yelling,
the thousand year treks.
I'd like to prop my weapon
against a tree in the desert
and make love with you,

see if I still remember,
or even knew, how.
Some days we're rowdy pigeons,
some days doves.
Someday I'll let it all go

like a flock to scatter
and rest in open fields.
Until then I may have forgotten
something really important.

I Have Only
with longing for Kate's red tail hawk

I have only to get on this airplane,
only a few small items as once before.
If we come down on the edge
of *water without end*, the golden rolling hills
and eucalyptus dream; if we touch down
I will open myself again to you.
I have only to present my ticket.

If this is the coast of my youth
I will make a blessing by scattering
handfuls of sea skyward
saying, Well done, then.
Well done, now.
I won't drop to my knees,
or maybe I will.

Forty years ago in an unplanned exodus
a spirit accompanied us
out of The City, south
on a crooked string hugging the rocks,
beckoning through mist.
Always ahead of us, her blueness
sudden in fog, kept us on course.
They walked among us then.
I have only this assent.

I work from memory—
the sky appears in patches
beneath our feet; jail cells

are twined with morning glories
and psychedelic breakers;
a writers' nest hangs over the cliff;
a boy becomes a man he can't yet see.

Nothing agrees, everything is lined up
with lights along the spine, the wild path
never far from itself. California,
if you are still willing
I have only to unravel
my tattered rug on this sand.

Where the Gulls Sleep

Bougainvilleas twine
high enough to see the sea,
its bank of unpredictable fog,
its song of restless heaving.
A single crow, urgent and alone,
caws out of habit
for all the moons
that have come and gone.

She says some blooms
are so fragile they can't
lift their own head,
while the automatic lights
and the automatic fountain
expect an automatic response.
Developers have fornicated
in these flower beds.
From here, she says,
I can hear the ocean.

We stand in the garden
and I wonder
if it's really the breakers
or just the traffic of her family
pulling her back into the street.
But she knows
the feel of her own tide,
where the gulls sleep.
She's no stranger
to night blooming jasmine.

At dusk she watches the herder's dog
put the sheep in the barn.
She sleeps curled next to the sea.
When she leaves,
as habit says she must,
I throw back the drapes,
let the moon
have what's left.

LATE SUMMER

It falls faster now,
down from the top of summer
where the sun eased over the edge
of the longest day, the mouth of the world
opened as wide as it could.
It falls fastest toward the lip
of a blue bowl. It falls now

through tiers of leaves
and the branching dancing arms
of her hallelujahs.
    I too am on my way,
arriving again and again
with no attachment to flags—
a red shirt today, white tomorrow.

But I know the function
of clothing, the skin I wear,
    the one that wears me,
buttons north and south
along the spine of this drum.

Flies drift slow in the in between;
squash and melons crown in my field.
I am here, close to myself, a song
all around me, naked silence poised
with everything to say.

If I must say what I am, then
today I am this turning, a wave
gushing in a knot, a sigh
    going out to sea.
Soon I will be equal.

GETTING THE PRAIRIE INTO PERSPECTIVE

Laramie—I was lonesome there
but I didn't need to be.
West of Medicine Bow dry snow
    hides out in the folds
of Rattle Snake Hills, but other than that
moisture is just an old story they tell
to chase away the sound of clattering bones.

The rails are cold, but still buzzing
    where east met west
and Hidatsa footprints disappear
into the dust of long gone buffalo.
I huddle over a gas hose.

The bleak and reckless sun,
or the dark clouds of early December—
either way—it's a temptation
to go mad. Go ahead,
pull your collar up,
but the wind will still find you
    like a dusty swirl of
last year's chamisa blooms.

I'm looking to put my hands
around a warm cup of smooth-waisted coffee.
I'm learning to substitute.

By late afternoon I drop
down into Colorado. The peaks there
are gold and guarded; the Front Range

is a prostitute coping with violation.
I had no idea
    what destitution was
until I entered that opulent sprawl.

I could turn around,
take Happy Jack Road,
be standing in the middle
of a familiar nowhere by nightfall.
I could practice gratitude
like a kangaroo mouse sniffing at snow.

WAKING THE BIG BLUESTEM

"Everything's different since you white people went to the moon."
—<u>Seeing Into Stone</u>, Katherine Park

When the sod bustin' began
I went deep into the dirt,
the rows clawed there
      across her face.
I find no place in their holy book
for the tall grass prairie.

No place for cone flower;
no place for buffalo
or even for their own children,
      save as objects
into which they plow
their orderly expectations.

I do not honor their treaties,
      anymore than they do,
but for different reasons.

This is the prairie
gone to sleep at our feet.
This is my heart
waiting out the drought of their dream.
This is the tall, tall grass
      before any of us came.
This is the singing prairie, long,
long after those people are gone.

ENTERING IN

We're done with nailing him up,
done with running her through
with the industrial shaft
of a runaway bus.
We're done with stories
of the stage, veils and masks.

What story can crack this sky?
What myth of water
could be better than
a cool, clear drink?

I see hands.
I see hands reaching in.
I see the village
shaping itself in blue-green wonder,
a fragment of red thread
writing itself through the air.

The new curricula will count
the weight of each and every soul.
Halleluiah is inherent here.

The trees have stood by us.
The whales, mushrooms, ants.
We witness one another, enter in,
unravel in this seed pod sky.

EYE OF DEPARTURE
December 21ˢᵗ

Converging at the dark point,
at the almost everlasting of it,
at winter's eye of entry
and departure, all
the voices of myself crowd
    into this small room.
Some reconciliation has occurred.

Disparate aspects walk
as one. The masks
of *hurry* and *wait*
    now wear a face
of mild anticipation.
Others, *aloof* and *overbearing*,
share the couch but eye
one another with familiar caution.

But not everyone need be chummy here—
what's a Solstice party
without some degree of edge?
The wind and the snow scream
and fight in midair;
a hawk holds a sparrow
to the cold branch, tears
tendons from hollow bone.
    All is well
as we pass through.

What has been fixed
and what has been abandoned
will be revealed in thaw's return.
A Santo Niño candle
flickers until dawn.

Enough to be the Earth

Underneath the dreams
of fulfillment and demise,
beyond the breakers

where no boat rocks or plies,
so deep into the nothing of now
that even the hum

of far star nurseries
opens wide, there I
can find no name.

Nothing written.
This body or the next
you have believed

will touch and feel and know.
This body of wanting and dividing
and dying, this body

we think and then we see,
this lovely, tragic marble at spin—
must she be everything?

Unsuspected Compañeros

HUDDLED AGAINST THE MOON

Grounded now in the beef
of altercations, in the sugar
of Christmas parties, in the
unholy finance of fear,
I mistake myself for the discomfort,
for this *experiencias* I wear.

Winter's moon is close
but untouchable. You're gone—
shopping.
Want and denial dance together.

I've changed my name
more times than I remember
and still the trees
are silent, their blood
slower but roaring

while leaves unfurl
and fall as before.
Are you the *unreturned*,
or shall I learn to wait
in this notch of northern shadow?

Flight Carries Its Own Current

It would be easy to call
them savages, the way
they raise exotic birds, gazelles,
even babies of their own kind
to shoot them there
on the run. But moreover
I must say *immature*.
　　These metal bangers,
these fire benders—
their siege cannot last.

All day long I drop my cap,
find it, lose it again.
All day long I tear
through the streets, distracted,
going through the trash,
trying on faces in the shops.
　　All day long
I hum in silence. . . to myself.

Peace could know itself
on a day like this.
I had been propping it up
like some fragile wing—
I was wrong.
My effort had been sustaining lies:
the entertainment of politics,
the guilt of breaking the egg.

My hands wring themselves

as I pass through the news,
those stories stacked like cards
to resemble a house.
When I'm stubborn, my brother
brings me back.

All day long
I kick along the shore
    or hover here;
this parade of questions and time
passing under the bridge,
this pervasive humming
    like an ocean,
this updraft over the coast.

As They Said
for Mary riding the Van

It was, as they said, a job
and I went to it.
So much cutting and stacking,
reams of paper—reams, I tell you.
Subordinates, overlords,
the ordinary pipsqueaks.
Was I a mistake?

I laddered the falls.
I was tabled and chaired.
I brown-sacked my communion.
I got my name in those papers.

The collusion of the stasis of the power
of the pretending of the preposition without end
was wearing thin. Where
were the stone streets without theme;
where were the fireflies?

I knew enough to know
that this was my hammer on the sill,
my rivet gun, my hard hat
and blood on the plans.
It wasn't always so—there must
be a world outside this one.

It wasn't like I didn't know any angels.
I'd grabbed my soul by the collar
and pulled it up close:

Listen here, buster,
this is an in and an out;
we secure the asset and head for home.

Out the window steady-eyed pronghorns
faced east, web-footed friends
came in at an angle.
Someone knocked—it was the wind.
Even the clouds looked
mildly amused at my little bubble.
A river surged on my left, on my right.
The hills heaved.
It was not as they said!

The line of the road gave way to
patterns, collisions, thunder.
Some greater engine was pulling.
Spring—I hadn't missed it!
I wanted to know
which trees had set their buds.
I wanted to touch someone.

GETTING DOWN TO IT

Getting down to the green of it
we side stepped our own homelessness
while bulldozers tore at kitchen gardens.
Getting down to the green of it
we clutched our hollow wanting
just below the navel, just above
the house of everyone posturing,
the TV dream streaming.

Getting down to the green of it
we caught the sins of our parents, tried to love
their crookedness, our eyes covered with three dollar bills.
Getting down to the green of it
we taught ourselves to hear the dove
deep in the bird, to lean out
past the textbook machine.
Getting down to the green.
Getting down to it.

Getting down on a mattress,
on the grass across summer's lawn,
on a car seat so quiet in the side yard.
Getting down to you and me, and then some.
Getting down we pulled on the ropes,
raised our sails, let our freak flags fly.
Getting it on, we got down.

Getting down to the green of it
we spun on our heads,
danced until we were tan, until we were

tough and dust and pulsing
with the drum of the earth.
Getting down to the dirt of it.
Getting down.

Getting down we kicked out the rows
and made a circle, the old ones, the children,
the rainbow conference.
Getting down to the green of it
we lifted our hearts as proof of humanity,
its beating the beacon of liberty.
Getting down, we get to the green of it.

To Cast Another Dawn

When the lights came
all the way on
it didn't matter
which way I was facing.

I could have caught
the light everywhere.
Caught it along the skin
or in the seed, caught it

where we meet, in the flame
above your head.
When the lights came on
the difference between us was:

show me yours—show you mine.
Our different shapes delight,
born all from sound.
The balancing on razor's edge,

the slam-dunk danger
and dark corridors were just
the honest work of rigging the sails.
This day was made

for sailing—and the night
with its starry net for pulling in
the orphan light
to cast another dawn.

Slip It

This velvet maroon bookmark
from Lummox is tucked, gold embossed,
a sidewinder's scepter.

I'm pulling it like a pistol
from colors talking in tongues.
I'm heaving like a sidewalk

due south, shattering on this page.
I'm looking for a place to slip it:
the demon gospels of Jesus,

the cleavage of Revelations.
This dark velvet across your collarbone.
This shadow where everything shines.

ICE BALL RETURNING
from the Roadhouse at Starvation Mesa

I didn't come late but I came after, after
Rick and Rain Dog had
tuned up with the Chicken Man,
came after the original sidewinders—
the living: Macker, Murray, Amalio and Levering;
after the deceased, of whom we speak,

and who speak through us—speak now
as *calaveras* simmering deep in the red,
as unsuspected *compañeros*
offering soul cakes to expiring artists
on the slopes of Starvation Peak.

I came in time
to hear the bell, to pet the dog,
to find the glow inside, to put a hand
on the next shoulder over, to feel one on mine.
Lineage of the badlands.

In one life alone, I've known
the reclamation of wasted winter,
washed out bridges on stretches of Old 66
and further north on 666. I've known
two sets of bathrooms or none at all
and too damn many nights curled up in County.

I didn't so much mind the dust
and the lopsided shingle, but

doubting the dream was certain hell.
I've been looking for this roadhouse.

I've been late for class, late for dinner,
and late for death;
I've been slow to pull and slow
to get the essence of her complaints.
It's a fact: I just don't straighten up good.

Tonight the mojo doctor was in, and I
stumbled across the threshold,
my little poems scattering,
so much kindling I guess.
I was mostly just a lot of appetite—
the appetite of a far flung comet
entering the orbit of outlaw poets, the blues
calling lost sons back to the fire,
fusing hot iron with emptiness.

I'm vapor. I'm Voodoo. I'm luminous.

MAKIN' THE ROUNDS
for the lonesome boys

In the city they walk their dogs
in ones, twos and threes;
every poem's a timed event.

Upcountry they laugh
in the back of the truck.
Some dogs stay gone for years.

Hell, it takes that long to make the rounds.
Make 'em now outlaw. Make 'em wide
by way of Anton Chico, wide
by way of Lindrith and Amalia.

Make it to the Line Camp, to the Mine Shaft;
    have one on Diablo.
I'm saying goodnight and hello
with a soft growl. I'm swinging wide
but I'm on my way home.

When you're upcountry your life's
    a sand painting
blowing in the wind. Then
the girls come traipsing in,
but not like before.
You've got to sift through bits
of turquoise and your own confession;
you've got to step around
the ant hills.

Those sandy trails
are for star-eyed coyotes
and the going-home dogs.
Go on, now. Go home.

From the top of the ridge
I'm what's left of the moon
    saying goodnight
through your broken window.

GRIEF

It's time for the hill,
for that coyote thing.

Time to crawl,
bleed into the ground,
into the stars, into the cold—
get my bleeding done
before dawn.

We're here on the hill,
nevertheless alone,
bleeding spots everywhere,
each coyote to his own.

In the morning, this red hill.
In the morning, just men
on their way back to work.
Some dust, some swirls.
    Just a hill
where some howling went down.

BLUE VOICE
for Tony Moffeit

I reach for a voice
but not just any voice, maybe
a blue voice, maybe
the voice of sharpened steel
fashioned in the shop, sweat dripping
onto the stone, the noon whistle
far and gone, that five o'clock shrine.
The voice of night thick
with car radios and bra straps,
crickets and night hawks far into it.
The voice of sawdust shuffling,
of come here and go away and I'm so sorry.
Whiskey voice.

A Cherokee voice, a cotton voice,
a county jail cell voice,
the last voice standing on the bridge,
the voice of dirt hitting a box.
Jerry Lee's voice, Woody's voice,
Jimmy, Zimmy, a coal miner's daughter.
A voice saying You're not welcome here,
a voice saying Come on in.
a box of voices to get through customs,
a boundary of voices, whatever accent
gets you on down the line.
Any voice without blame.

I reach deep for a voice,
deep into the black soil

and sandy bottoms, deep
into the blues man gravel, scratchy records.
The voice of America—God damn you.
This voice telling you
to get your business straight,
this voice ripping out my heart,
putting it on the block for you.

This voice in need of a mouth, this voice
in need of ears, this voice
yipping into the wind.
The voice of overworked rivers
crying dirty tears, the voice of mountains
catching rain and bulldozers
and the deafening hell of dynamite.
Your voice and mine.

Your voice on scraps of paper hung with the drum,
your voice from Claremore to Pueblo.
Her voice over and over again
on the answering machine.
Your junkyard voice with clanging gates,
your five hundred dollar hospital plates.
I am also that voice.

I'm the voice of wanting
too much and not enough.
I'm the voice of belonging
stumbling through this empty night.
I'm the voice of the mother
pulling back the sheets on this wreck
calling for the children,
sifting through tornadoes.

I'm the urgent voice, the soothing voice,
the long gone lonesome voice,
voice without end,
voice without end,
voice of the mute angel and surviving wind,
this blue voice.

No Sidestepping This One

A sandy, wide river
drains the Rockies, sways
across the plains, chances a run
through eastern Oklahoma.
My grandmother MacGregor
made that run in '92—
horses, dust, rifle shots,
precious things wrapped
    in precious cloth.
The hand-painted plates, the mirror.

I wasn't there, not then.
I was born into air-conditioning,
Sputnik, McCarthy. I was
a boomer with food on the table,
father's uniforms hanging in the hall,
    black and white re-runs
of the invasion.

When I looked up the people
had fallen silent.
When I looked up I saw
clouds scattered like deer;
the Chickasaw, the Kickapoo
    also thinning.
I saw how this deal works.

My people settled next to the river,
below the hill. Tornadoes
left us alone because of it—

that's what the Osage said.
    Where I've walked
is what rolled over those old ways.

You don't have to
wash mouths out with soap
to say you voted for progress.
    Your every step
splits the world in two.

SWEAT BEADS

> "The Speaker of the House can be found
> on certain, but not all, beads of the Rosary."
> —Robert Reeves

As if you could hear yourself through the clamor; as if
this phone card was good; as if the potter had put
a secret spin on each drop of blood.

Yesterday, or some other legal description,
I tumbled these rosewood beads in a bowl of sand.
I came forth, just like they said.
I'm a Hand Trembler from Kayenta. I'm holy on the horizon.
What is your question? You see,

already you're the one with an answer. Now,
get out of here, I've got a desert to walk.
My hand trembles from handling
too many, just too damn many.
Can't you see I'm working here?
As if you might know which one

leads to the fifth island;
as if redemption was a bone you could
put your finger on; as if we could pretend
there was no connecting thread.
Cut this cord,
spill all the planets in a row
across the dark and fleeting hand of night.

COMPLETELY NAKED GOES TO NEW YORK
a sugar cube of American history

You merged with the algae world.
After taking off your clothes
time and again
you finally got naked
in a high meadow.
Water welcomed you then.

Old friend, it said, finally
one has come that listens;
we are one here
though the waves are many.

Later you stood
on the rear platform of the bus
and showed truckers
the true curve of the world,
the chilling warmth
and depth of skin.
You let your garment fall.

The stars were tracking you. Evidently
you're a prankster when you say you are.
Further is not a distance;
it's a bus.

THE DRIVER

I came a little before dawn,
turned the corner, looked in.
He was waiting. I noticed
some setback had left him
gimpy on the inside, the kind
of wobble and tilt that said
he'd put his time in on the farm,
plowing and raking in the midday sun,
bewildered and a bit blindsided
by the repetition of lightning.

He'd come through it just fine. . .
though he didn't necessarily think so.
      But I wasn't there to judge.
      I drive the van.
They're either ready or not.
That's the joke on the team: *Ready or Not.*
You can't get too caught up in this shit.

Granted, it's not the drama of EMS.
Those guys are dealing in *time*,
disfiguration, last minute stuff:
 Yes — No — Maybe —
people still believing in debt.
Hey, I just take 'em out
to the countryside.

You'd be surprised—or maybe you wouldn't—
how many people get really nervous
without car keys, blame, smartphones, obligation.

And all those *freakin'* life forms running around.
You'd think they'd had this jewel
all to themselves.

So at first I keep to the hills,
familiar things: oak trees,
robins, sparrows, sparrows.
After all,
that wide horizon can be
way too much all at once. Besides,
their home star comes into view
soon enough *and that*, my friends,
is when the small talk stops.

THE ZERO OF IT

Go deep, go dark,
go to the zero of it.
Paint the names of God
in blood; paint them here
on the dirty lace of seaport towns
where rats throw craps
and queens break heels.

Paint over the shops of masks
and manufacture of containers.
Nothing is artificial.
All is holograph.

Go wide, go blind,
go to the hum of it.
Cast your fate
in forward acts of remembrance;
direct your thinking
if thinking makes it so.
This is the last drop of ice,
the last sliver of indifference.

Holy is the way
it fountains from your head.
Sweet with fingers
is sunlight thrilling in the leaves.

American Poet

I don't want to be a poet anymore,
    not an American poet
with those American microphones,
American scorecards,
virtual friends, hours spent
in front of the mirror.

I don't need a shoe
that's a color no one else has,
a device that reminds me
that I'm "liked". Anyway,
which revolution is this?

Tell me something
    that will never be on TV,
something that has the cut
of your street, but not
that singsong pause and punch.
Tell me what you plan to do
with your new found poverty.

I want to write in chalk, read
to passing birds, discard poems
    pre-production.
There is no stage, just water
to distribute, and mouths,
so many dry mouths on the desert
trying to swallow sound bites.

WE GO UP IN THE SAME FLAME
after Vassar Miller

You die of fire and I of burning.
In character, or out, I recognize
the heat within us.
But if there is one longing

it has many names—
longing for a high school love,
for clean water, for legs.
Longing for warmth, the sleep of ice,
for the sky to rest, to mend.

Something to eat.

Manuelito, you left Juarez
where they kill one another
over drugs going north, with guns
given in my name. Longing
is the shape of a family
all together at the table,
spending their pay on corn,
not on coffins.

Longing is a flame
I keep in my window. This burning
of borders, this fire between us.
There's room for you here. Here
there is also burning.

SOMEONE SWEET
SHOWED ME THIS DIRT

Santa Barbara Canyon in Autumn Rain

Damp gold leaves, fir, spruce,
pine needles, moss.
All is soft in mist:
faces, hands, thoughts, thirsty rock.

The twert of a distant bird,
    forest companion
beneath a canopy of heliotropic reach.
Daises come out in the rain.

On a fallen log words seep
onto your notebook. We part.
The path calls me further,
feet only to feel—not a sound.

I move on moist air.
I'm a secret tree detached,
    travelling among friends.
They greet me as a spirit.

At the spring—thrushes, maiden hair fern.
The river is a choir of clouds
and the sea falling in single file.
This shimmering pool; my invisible wings.

Sunset on Silver Avenue

A quilt of pigeons
   unwraps and turns
      in a pale pink winter sky—
         light, dark, invisible.

Reappeared, they settle
   on the roof, ignore
      the plastic owl and frenzy
         of last-minute shoppers.

A light comes on. . . two more.
   Inside the girls shake it up
      with guitar and tambourine.
         You look for an empty chair

while boyfriends video
   the whole thing on phones.
      The pigeons blink and coo
         and tilt their heads.

Their soft brown talk
   is almost a whisper now.
      Soon the street
         will be all there is.

Round Trip on the Rail Runner
sketch from a train traveling on time

With torn breath
and hands in pockets we look
for the piercing light. Then
the dry ditches of winter,
the spurs into gravel lots,
the hand-signed sunsets
of backyard visionaries—
it all begins to roll,
rear cars catching up on the slow.

So called salvage—
you could pick up half this town
with a magnet, the other half
with a lost soul catcher.
You could buy another ticket
at Alvarado Station but you must
leave the rails
to make the walk up Tomé Hill.
I'm one stop short of my own whistle.

The blown out windows
of our fathers' industry
and determined farms of *pobladores*
call mice and cranes back
to the homes of their evacuation.
But love prevails, its evidence
in the smoke of crooked stovepipes
and mittens on the line.
There's a wide river here.

The trains runs on time.
The stations have digital read-outs;
the porter carries a watch.
When the doors close
time paces the platform,
waits for another chance.
This tube travels like a carriage:
colonial, upright, suspended.

We unwrap tamales, pass
the jug, counterfeit tickets.
Somebody unlocks their bike;
somebody deals with the drunk.
A baby behind me glees "Choo choo,"
a reference probably
from a pasteboard book, after all
this train howls like a future hound
avoiding impact.
We're all part of this same dream—
dividing neighborhoods
or getting grandpa to the 4:16.

East Mountains in new snow
hold deep shadows, stories
of advance and retreat.
The land gives up anything
if you ask with a sharp enough shovel.
Rust and mud and mist
are testimony to the way it takes.

Our shadow is long now
in the fields; our shadow
is sharp across the water.

From Los Lunas to Isleta
we lose the light, aware
of ourselves on the return trip
as faces in a window, dots
on the rim of a pot, the dogs
too busy to look up.

SUMMER THIS
at San Yasidro de Corrales Parish

The sadness of summer all around us—
    the fullness of it.
Another red juicy thing
bringing us to our knees,
flowers turned to beans.
One by one young bunnies slip
into the mouths of coyotes,
the hot black center of the Milky Way, just there
in the tail of Scorpio, rotating,
singing at the seams.

At sunset we stroll
through the old cemetery, the one
relocated after the flood, some red gravel
scattered for a path, cottonwoods feeding
on what the worms have prepared—
everything above ground, in the open.
No mysteries in crumbling tombs
or fading flags.

The work of redemption is being done
by families of woodpeckers
upside down and sideways
as they tease at twisted limbs.
    What is growing is green,
or nearly so: buffalo gourds, tumbleweed.
Even the sand that's shifting
at the feet of plaster virgins
believes only in this moment.

With Lunasa a quarter moon away,
summer strains at the strings.
What is not picked, will rot—
and certainly that is a kind of eating.

All the urge of getting ready,
and all the dying afterwards
    for this,
this one ripe summer afternoon.

[ANOTHER] LOS ALAMOS FIRE

I've left my skin on those rocks.
From Cochiti to Canoñes
those *barrancas* have saved me
from the ordinary, the pavement
and underground atomics, from
disregard and lack of music.

They say the forest is on fire
as if that one word were the sum
of Indian Paintbrush, Monks Hood,
patches of lichen holding their breath
into the rolling blaze.
As if I wouldn't feel
each clump of rice grass as it joined
bluebirds and cracking ponderosa
in the hereafter of New Mexican sky.
I know those brown boulders.

The sharp edges and false entries
of the Pajarito Plateau,
like a broom skirt saying *No*,
kept the Conquistadores at bay.
My love, my sanctuary.

A hundred miles away I breathe
the bitter butterscotch
and delicate Sweet Clover sigh,
a letter of goodbye arriving
on late afternoon wind. Already
my streams are choked with fallen deer.

I could not be there
at the moment of your ascension.

I will not light a candle for you—
enough of fire!
My well has shrunk to a trickle.
I will sit with you in the dark
and together feel the welling dryness.
I will let my tears fall
next to your orphaned seeds.

Driving Home from Christmas Dinner
for Nancy and Lindsey Enderby

The God blessedness of it;
the howling viola
and smiling dog of it;
the beauty that sets fire
to the wind.
I've already caught you;
Go ahead—fall, she says.

The light sweeping down
Taos Canyon, shadow
following close behind;
the night with its mouth open
all the way home.
We should wonder
at the magic of ourselves.

When I leave the blindfold on
I can tell you how she moves.
I know that you also
marvel at her ways.

The junipered dunes in snow.
A crescent moon for Christmas.

Tonight that band
of melon-colored light lay
between the darkening blue
and volcano's silhouette,
a goodbye arc roaring

silently round the earth.

Like an outlaw whisper
I circle the fire.
Your name crackles
in the embers. Here
there is not one mistake.

THE SUN HERE
for Julie Brökken

We've spoken of the Alvarado Station
but today I prefer to sit
in the sun with vendors,
fine Indian jewelry, chewing gum.
The Number 3 is running
a half hour early with you
returning from winter oats,
from soy and polled cattle,
from rolling farms and families still
heaving in the heat of the frontier.

Rivers are wide there, you report,
on fire at night as they pass through cities.
You'll hit open sky
on the morning of the second day,
run alongside the Old Santa Fe Trail.
You'll catch a bobcat in your camera.

In a foreign restaurant with Ketchup
on the menu a woman
watches train wrecks on a smartphone
for no apparent reason—it's a wonder
we keep this dream together at all.

This afternoon I need the hum of the rails.
I need to stand close
to my expanding heart.
I need just a little more highway
to get this healing done.

East of town Sandia Peak
shimmers unreal, a Gaussian blur
as cranes glide in over
Witchweed and Swamp Willow.
Then the whistle, the headlamp,
the brakemen, the flagmen on the tracks,
travellers moving toward the sound.
A refugee steps down, coming home
from the United States.

This sun has no need to be smart.
People here still follow it.

SANTUARIO REPLACED

It's become its own slot machine.
The majick has moved on. Requiem indeed.
I went to Chimayo on Friday.
    Autumn is an iron bell tied to my heart.

Be wary of words that don't rust,
come full circle with the sand on your shoe.
They leave the fruit to rot on the trees.
    The majick has moved on. Requiem indeed.

How many crutches can we hang?
Another store—then another one.
Who has the most faceless friends?
    Come full circle with the sand on your shoe.

Before I'm green, I'm yellow again.
There's a garden here somewhere.
Someone sweet showed me this dirt.
    Another store—then another one.

This river is full of stones.
The rain always comes from above.
I go out back and wash my hands in the stream.
    There's a garden here somewhere.

They tie their crosses to the fence.
Autumn is an iron bell tied to my heart.
I, too, will be moving along.
    The rain always comes from above.

JEMEZ

I go north into red rock, eat bread
fried over fire, find the layered land,
consider the dust—all
that has been formed in dust,
for dust, with dust. A white eagle
hovers over the mesa; the wind blows,
but just so much.

A grandma knocks a little shoe
against the leg of a chair,
shakes red dirt on the ground,
ties it snug on his foot, then the other.
I'm at home with quiet words.

At the base of a sediment cliff
yellow flowers run a ways, then
stop in a curve. Swirls of ancient water
made little holes where
single-note birds come and go.
One of them seems to know me.

Some happiness has descended,
or risen—anyway,
location is not what we thought.
My hand rises without prompting
as I'm reminded
to wave at travellers, those
holy shapes and forms,
this grand migration of ours.

At the place of wrinkled earth
a gray jut of solidified sea
forms a dam, diverts canyon water.
Tang of sulfur mixed with
ragweed, marsh grass, delicate asters.
Bird shadow races across ant-walked rock.

A man struts to the edge, grinds
his cigarette on soda stone, returns
to wife and camera and steering wheel.
I find little to say to him
that would be helpful.
Beautiful day. Perhaps
that white agate worn smooth
will talk to him in a way
that gets his attention.
It can be a slippery path
when the stone weeps.

When the mountain comes up
I go to the top—
crows and colors and rifles cracking,
the usual phenomena. I wait
as instructed, then come down
to smell the cows
on their way to market, to see
who has bloomed in the meadow.

The men come home with their shovels.
They finished these tunnels
a hundred years ago,
so don't be surprised if you see me
growing from steep rock, see me growing

where young couples hunt
for waterfalls, and autumn sumac
cascades like fire.
I know these songs by heart.

KACHINA, EMERGE

You there, shaking corn at the sun,
bending over wavy lines of water;
you, burnt sienna and rusty blood peeling
from the plastered walls preserved
in the conqueror's museum,
consider this before you continue
into the dream that is my now—

We have more metal
where this came from; we have
a trade fair dependent
on perpetual war; we have fires
at night that will find you
around any corner.
We have warehouses. . . full.

We destroy a thing, then
wonder at its value.
We say we are not afraid
of lightning. We lie out of habit.
Our babies are beautiful
but bewildered. We dance
for gold with permanent feathers.

Study us long and hard
before you enter, but believe nothing
you think you see. Kachina,
whirling from the earth,
when you covered yourself in dust
I mistook it for defeat.

I am Myself in the Swirling Eddy

Because I step aside,
    appear to hover here
next to this clack of wet bones,
do not mistake my love
of this walk, this way,
concrete or pine needled path.
I know these rusty nails,
mild peach blossom winds,
touch of her cheek.

I can smell the sea
a thousand miles away.
I have a knee that sings of rain,
a finger that twitches when
the roar of the sun leaves its perch.

Circle my town in a single day;
spend a lifetime
    with this moon.
Someone planted this tree;
someone cried at this river
as the cranes passed overhead.
I pretended that these roots
belonged only to you.
You pretended it too.

But there's no denying it: my skin
is mixed with the brown silt
    swirling here;
my feet are fast in this ground.

From Here I Stand

I must speak for myself
on these matters. I have no armies standing
behind me on the banks of this river.
Bullets and words whiz every which way.
I say for myself what I see.
    I say for myself where I go.
The Blue Coats, the Red Coats;
the Grey Coats, the Green;
my family with feathers in their hair.

I am on the side of deer
bedded down beside the water.
I am on the side of all that must migrate.
I am on the side of a hill
that will heave again with red hot sun.
    I eat what I kill.
Show me your long knife
and I will show my taste for you.

I cannot be your friend
if friendship calls for religion, the religion
of "Woe Is Me," the religion
    of "Us and Them,"
the religion of zombie conquest.
I have stood in the circle
and I have walked away.
I have circled the world
and I stand where I stand.

Brothers and sisters, I will call you,

not because we have the same handshake
or credit card, not because I am in need
    of your tattoo or vote,
but because—all that bleeds will wake,
and all that wakes is one.

I am on the side of deer standing
    in tall grass.
Can you not see that
we are dancing?

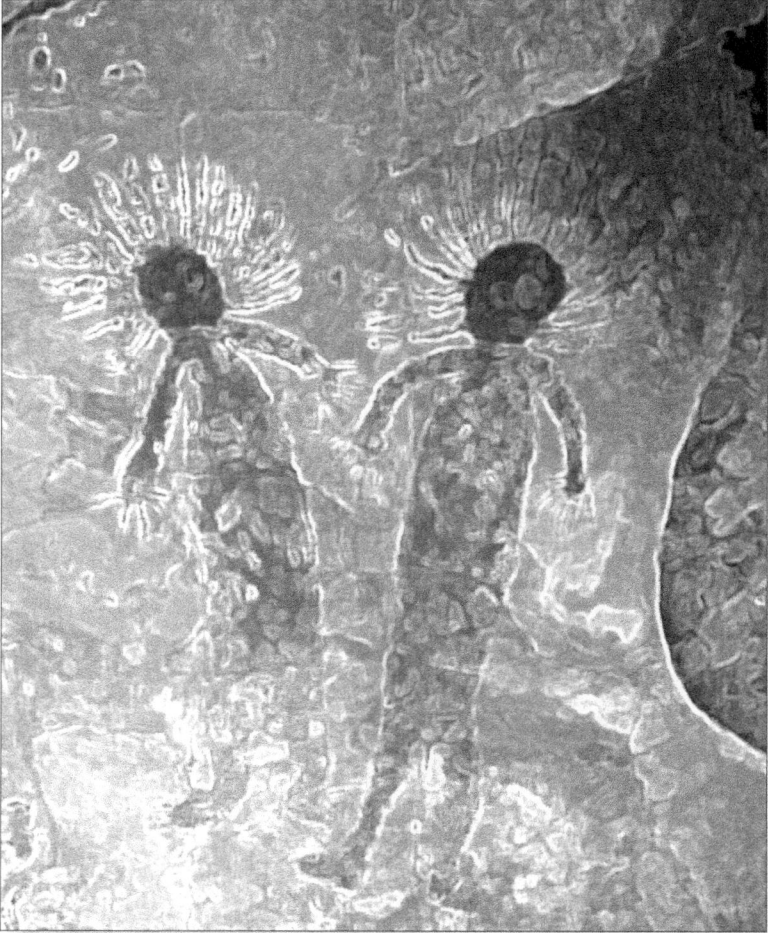

A Bell Has Found Us

THE MOUNTAIN COMES FOR HER
for Lauren

The dust, she says,
is different here, the dust
with light inside, the dust

of this new land old
with the spent clothes of souls
lifting in the wind.

I am an image developing
on the face of western clay.
I am arrived, and yet a witness.

I speak dialects
from the islands: Cuba,
Miami, Manhattan. I speak

and hold my tongue.
What this dust knows
is what I need.

Nights here are tossed
in the claw
of the moon.

I'm ready for love, she says,
I'm not afraid
of this wind.

My Beloved

She stands in pose, begins
  in saffron, bends to the sun
    as child, as tiger, as downward dog.

We're doing parallel play.
  I'm holding energy in the word *starbound*,
    releasing it in the next line.

She attends to ankles, breathes
  into old dreams, stiff memories. Bliss
    rolls out one vertebrae, two, three...

Just notice, the teacher says—just notice.
  An orange is peeling across the page.
    Now she's an ocean. The horizon

is lost, reappears. All is close, vast, undulating.
  I am a seagull crying for rocks,
    naming the breakers. Her breath

is one holy door after another; her fingers
  speak with trees, lift as wings.
    We turn at the same moment.

A bell has found us facing east,
  this ringing without beginning,
    this dusty road falling for the sea.

Protected Lands

Is this the valley scorched so
long ago, trace of charcoal,
cracked and scattered stones?
Is this the numbness of the earth
after the blast, the wind
looking for what's left?
I am not a stone, she says.

Not wholly of this world, your human half
stirs, begins to grow—repair.
Star charts are no use in stormy weather,
only the keel of emotions
to steady the gusts on the sail.

In the office they play Yes Sir, No Sir,
blow each other down, get it done right.
In the forest birds don't have names
but nevertheless say hello—all day long like this:
Hello humans, hello. One day
you answer. Look up

from your paper and plan,
they move from tree to tree.
This is not the fourth planet, but the third.
Fireflies, seeds on the wing, green things
anxious to come back.
Roots, my love, after all.

THE COURSE OF IT

This morning—waves building
in some other ocean, love with sand
between its toes. Here, the warmth
of the singular sun.

Saturday—A light breeze taking away
finch poop in glittering ribbons,
February's snow dissipating,
a romance breaking on the shore.
A swell wave it was.

Last Tuesday—Seating is limited.
I put on an orange jump suit and enter
in handcuffs. It's the only way
it can be about me *too*.
She comes prepared.

An important holiday—Unfinished business
before sunrise hammers hard
against my window. It has nothing
to do with her—but I forget
to send a heart shaped poem. Uh oh!

Three weeks ago—White caps glisten;
we hold our hearts to the sun.
It works best when I hold hers higher.
A shape breaks the surface.
I'm in love.

January—A bright-eyed wind
gathers on the open sea,
star charts unfurl, I hear
a bell deep in the night, a bird
returns with a twig.

Last year—Adrift in doldrums,
fishing is slow. I remind myself the ocean
is mighty, it gives and it takes
as it will. Something moves here
without a stir.

ROMANTICISM

Whatever I did or didn't do
on Valentine's Day, it may not be over,
a storm that only pretends to pass.
I could repent, re-think,
see it her way.

I could carry her feelings,
carry them deep
in my pencils and pens,
in my industry and effort,
    on this trail
of bumbling love.
I could take responsibility.

She could tell me how, and
    for a moment
all would be well—
this invisible wound, this
untraceable harm
that we carry for one another.

IN A PARKED CAR

I have an idea—
let's be friends, I said,
    after pulling over
in a spot thinly shaded
by naked trees under a street lamp.

What words there were
had already been used, so I said,
I wasn't thinking enough of you;
I'm sorry you felt hurt.

But hurt, anger and disappointment
were feeling words.
    And that,
was where the cupboards seemed bare,
a house burnt nearly to the ground
by parents with flamethrowers.
You'd already walked out
on that part of yourself, so
how could anybody touch you there?

As your hand felt only
for the latch you said, Maybe
we should start tomorrow.

When the door opened
some cold rushed in, but the night,
the night finally had a feeling
that could be named—devastation.

Frost on Stones, Gulls Overhead
letter to Mary

I say that I live on the edge
of a lake. I say that I wander its shore
teasing small fires, meeting strangers,
exploring wrecks. In fact
I live on the third floor; the closest water
is my kitchen, after that
everything is seasonal and runs
in disappearing sheets or erratic rivulets.
I live on a high desert.
Sometimes I say I don't belong here.
I have learned to lie.
I say that I was married—
we'll leave it at that—details
can unravel into false memories.
The story of me (that could not love itself)
tried to love the story of her.
Somehow I believed that if we had stayed
we would have found the Maker of Stories
and let the lakeshore have its weather—
maybe not. If love is some treasure box
or arrangement, most mornings
I miss the ferry and have to stow away on a freighter.
If love is the wind at rest my breath
is testimony to constant wonder.
You remind me that this moment
can be finished, sufficient, needing
only a title, a piece of driftwood
placed against a rock.
You see the lake.

WAIT, I TELL THE DAY

Upturned clip of a moon,
low and ready to die
into the day. I wake
    as it slips south
around this mouth of mountain.

I've heard them speak
of the lovers' moon as a thief,

a witness, a confidant.
I've heard you ask
if I would wait six years.
I don't want the sun—
    not like that—
not another month without you.

Though she travels with it, how
could December's moon be enough
when the tide of my stars
falls toward Imbolc? Mary,
there is only this spring coming,

this one morning
to tear into the streets
calling for one another,
    slipping wildly
into the holy scheme before
    another dawn is gone.
Is that you I hear in the street?

Sun Shining Through
after the painting by Eric Wallis

When you reach back to tie
your hair out of the way
of morning's invitation
the light knows what to do.
Even the golden gladiolas
lean toward you. I too
want to stand near
your cool cheek, warm breath,
the stir of your soul making ripples.
We share the earth's sigh.

What I think I want is too much
or unimportant. There is nothing
I can make of myself for you.
I am caught in every lie.
The same sun is on my face.
What then should be our hurry?

I already know
the new green of this day,
how shadows are made
from red, these handfuls of you
under your white gown,
how my lips will brush
the nape of your neck.
I know teeth clear to the bone.

It doesn't matter what we play—
paint the kitchen, find the color,

dinner for two, for four, for thirteen,
dress up or down before bed,
movies on location. What
if we couldn't mess this up?

When you reach back
to tie your hair in the sun
it's none of my business
where your gaze goes. Mystery
must be allowed
to enter this canvas at will.

A Larger Togetherness

The soul, you say, is a friend.

My stories, my ragtag armies,
my congress of brittle sticks,
my orphanness—
they might all have to go
if what you say is true.
And what if our two souls
are friends; what then?

When I played as a child of five
with half buried bricks,
the cool soil holding them there,
the universe of underground bugs
and slow motion steps of a neighbor cat,
    someone else,
but not really an *other*,
was also there. In between

the peeping chatter
and spontaneous trills that later
I would call bird song
some *ongoingness*, some breath
without an in or out watched
    from everywhere.
We didn't speak,
though we might have.

If my not-so-secret friend
was there all along,
why not more than one.

And how do our souls converse,
    yours and mine
with one another, their
whale-like conveyances,
their unfathomable concern
diving deep with pups
in the ocean of our beginnings?

Storm Catching

Here, where the Rio Grande Uplift
gives way to the Sonoran Desert,
rain is an event.
We met like that: spark of lightning
between our cheeks when you leaned
close so not to disturb the audience.

You said your name
and I recognized it like a river
I had always wanted to walk. And now
in this flash flood
I didn't even hear the roar, caught
and tumbling before I knew it.
How can something so sudden seem so sure?

Sure, I've worked up and down the coast
where you can stand
in the slow drifting rain,
watch ferns unfurl and mushrooms bloom.
The rain there has constant companions;
sooner or later it know everyone.
They're not really storms,
and it's you who must decide
if the quiet dripping and constant mist are enough.
But the tall walking rain across the desert
can swing too wide, leave you
like a seed dry as a crack.

I suspect there's a mountain
where the rains meet to dance, do that

storming thing to their heart's delight.
Right about now, we're somewhere
in the foothills. Electricity all the way up.

From the Near Northeast

Sunrise happens
with a wide pallet knife,
dark strokes
left over right defining
an opening through clouds.
Not piercing star rays
or even its prologue,
nevertheless we roll
to face our assigned parent, the one
whose seed we replicate, replicate, replicate.
Ra, Sol, Savitra, ☉

The plaza has grown:
tiers of cement bridges
crisscross overhead,
the near deafening din
of trash being taken further out.
The pipes, the wires,
the conductorless trains.
It eats its way toward us.
Am I this humanity,
this clockwork virus?

This distance between us
is false, but I need you now.
I need flesh on flesh, your bangs
falling in your eyes,
your gloved hand and
your novel that will
bring us through the wreck.

I need you in me.

One day you will fold this school
like a cardboard stage; any moment
the bell will ring.

Sunset Walk in the Bosque

We found Clyde Tingley's boot
at the base of the trail all the way
from London, Ohio,
from the miles he walked for his wife,
from the republican butts he kicked
in the name of the New Deal.
We found it in layers
of fallen cottonwoods, red stem grasses,
water still and moving,
sun-tipped wings of geese.
We found ourselves

picking our way along the Rio Grande,
the streets of Albuquerque,
the pathways of our desire.
I don't want just any dream, you said.
I quoted some Dylan,
then commented on the hearth fires;
how the smell of smoke says a lot
about the neighborhoods. We passed
from red-heart cedar
through piñon and lesser pine
to cottonwood. Our gate slowed,

our stories like tree silhouettes against
the pale pink band of western sky
revealed our patterns, our
intent for spring.
You reached and took my hand.

It was easy then. We passed
by an old house, one of many
that had been a children's hospital
donated by Tingley. Some of these

large trees were also planted by him.
On Silver Avenue the sidewalk
went around one. The uneven ground
threw us closer together.
The birds, and even the dogs,
fell silent at the sight of Venus.

Angels Up Ahead

They appear as dots, tiny
as seeds, but when you talk
they connect—quadrillions
making curves in my mind
smooth enough to ride, to shine.
When you talk.

When you say words
I hear my exotic self,
mirror me, the female
I no longer have to be.
You've not stopped
at the story of skin; let's just say,
you're insatiable, or
some other word for eternity.

We can talk about it
two inches away (sweet vibrations)
or from the far backyard
of any galaxy. Meta-humanoid.

We can make children, you and me.
You've brought two beautiful beings
into the world: a girl, a boy.
You became the undulating earth,
the wet mouth of god
saying, *Aauumm.* Now

we can ignite thousands
in a joined thought.
When we talk.
They wait in love for us
in worlds yet to come.

WAY FAMOUS

My woman says, Let's be
way famous—after we're dead.
I agree; all this living to do.
When she curls up like a bloom
        on my chest spreading
as the rose ink of dusk across my sky
there is no digital attention
worthy of my distraction.
The world of divide and conquer be damned.

When she puts on her thin lips,
stands fist on hip I watch her take
        the horses out of the barn,
bring them back in satisfied lather.
When we both work for the undeniable sky
we takes turns wearing hats.

Late at night we're famous
on the couch; we're famous at the stove,
        at the letters between us,
our universities of imagination.
She's my home planet; beyond this
my lips are sealed with hers.

PROBE UNTIL A POOL APPEARS

IN THESE FIELDS

Tending the corn in this way
I follow the lights
up and down the stalk.
Nothing is random; all is chaos.
It works just fine.

And the way to know
the secret soil is to die,
to die like a leaf,
a rollie pollie, a VCR,
a pyramid, ocean wave.

I bring my body along, so much
water and wind slipping
through my grasp.
By the time I arrive only
these few thoughts.

If not this garment, then what,
    then who...
and who shatters this ear
from tassel to core?
These gold and purple kernels,
this reaching into rain.

WINTER'S DANCE

Deep into it we turn,
engage our opponent,
keep falling
toward the Ace of Shadows,
the solstice of it.

Memories of missing hands
and frozen teeth ghost
through our nakedness.
I've seen them before
in different versions of the village.
    Our mud faces,
        our house on fire.

We always torched it
when we were through.

I'm the ceremonial leader
of my own pageant;
I'm the night wind
below zero. Consider yourself
called into the circle.

STRIKE OF IMAGINATION

White without snow, without ash,
clean as a sink these late winter trees.
The wind laid down
sometime in the night,
is restless again.
    You think you need
to know something.

When am I a modern man:
when I juggle loves, manage
my hate and the news
of *Coca-Cola* owning rivers,
memorize a little baseball?

Tie a string to the thing
that wiggles in your dream
and you can say for yourself
who is teacher. Stick around,
it gets *different*.

A person, and not just someone,
has a spark that fits.
The trees are cold today
but only to the touch.
    You still know how
to start a fire in the wind.

LIFTING RIVERS, CATCHING RAIN

Sure, I know names for trees,
but what does it matter?
I've introduced these friends
as tossed against the sun,
as naked in their knowing,
as lifting rivers into the sky.
I've dropped to my knees
and raised my arms—
just as they do.

Whether I found this lodestone
or it found me
I don't know how to say.
Does the wind find the wing
or does the bird sing until it comes?
I turn this way, then
I turn this way.
As a stone I have much to say;
one syllable may last an age.

At *Caral* they found me
wrapped in cloth, buried
beneath my mother's floor.
At *Chichén Itzá* I jumped
into the sacred pool.
Why would I not return?
That smudge of unworthiness
worn on foreheads
washes off with the rain.

BROWN WOMAN WALKS

A brown woman walks at dusk,
hair tied back in a broom tail;
simple clothes, nothing really

to compete with the black and red birds
that call all day from tree to tree.
The pale horizon of mountain

returns its dream of star fire
to the night that leaves
only whisper lines floating.

She walks with a river's purpose
and though her feet touch the ground
and the birds have taken their places

in soft perched silence, the warmth
of her body leaves a trail
for the night moths and the angels.

She changes eyes with a blink, and prepares
for a night of seeing, this woman
who is brown disappearing, returning.

QUIET PLACE

You could cozy-in
on a day like this. Finally,
sheltered by snow clouds
and the relative quiet
of Sunday morning, you'd remember
seed pods and black stones
with white stripes wrapped
in red cloth, a piece of paper
with your other name
written phonetically in a friend's hand.

The cawing of that single crow
winging low through
the every-which-way
of winter branches would bring
meaning to this expanse
of otherwise high definition desert.
You could hear yourself sigh.

On a day like this
the whales would come in close.
Never mind what
you've been told about distance,
about scarcity or good looks.
What do they know
of migrations along a path of the heart?

Prayers have already been
made, set singing
on your forward course.

How else would you have known
to look, here,
in the quiet place?

OPEN HELLO

This is the door at which you stand
and fumble and stamp and fidget.
This is the door you've always passed.
This is the knock. This, the wait.
Which side are you on?

In the covered market of America
the door has been moved to the back,
tipped into the dumpster, taken
for a ride.
The hollowness of their eyes.
It's not your fault.

It's not your fault,
the false knocker, the pixilated frame.
I know a place where people
still say Hello. You know
that hello when you hear it.

This door opens into me,
into you,
this door we've dreamt together.
There is only one of us here.

Only this Ringing

There is no light.
Turn toward it now.

There is no road.
Take the path home.

There is no direction.
No body to call your own.

What Calls

It's not speculation
but true as the next wave,
next word, next breath.
Your future self.
Somewhere up ahead

in the knotted string of now,
in the flower that begins,
that becomes tomorrow's avatar
you beckon yourself forward. Life
does not regret itself.

I'm the leaf forming,
unfurling, falling from the sun.
I'm the place
where the tree used to be.
I'm nowhere at all.

To forgive is to know you
as myself. Your future, truly,
has no blame in it.
Tell me, who
is your best friend?

ONLY IF I TURN

Only if I turn
   toward the day; only
      if I suspect the sky.
         Only when the little bird sings.

Each falling leaf
   was too much death.
      Did I cause all this?
         Such a big idea for a small mind.

She takes me back like a brother.
   If I put my hand in the air
      I could say, This
         is where she lives.

Behind the song, a bird.
   Behind the bird,
      a breeze. I am breathed
      and I am breathing.

Only if I fall
   where the mountain falls.
      Only for the little bird
         do I listen.

As One

Less, I thought, and
as I thought it more
came by way of breathing,
by way of the overarching canopy,
snake dance dividing.
Of all people I was, I thought,
not the one to say
what was necessary, necessarily.

When my room turned
to the take the light it turned
with all the other rooms,
east-west streets, classrooms, cubbies,
the sides of everything sunning itself.
The shadows
made it seem that we were moving,
more or less. . .

DIG WHERE SHE SAYS DIG

This is where all the tracks disappear—
mine, yours, forward, back.
This is the sky swallowing us whole.

Unshoulder your pack, throw it down.
Toss that useless device.
   We're out of range.
Drop to your knees and start
digging—here.

How does the water move, where
is the sweet spot of her throbbing?
Pull up double handfuls of sand,
the roots of dreams gone to sleep,
a rusty thing, a shiny beetle,
the wetness of the earth.

Probe until a pool appears.
The birds—listen, the thirsty birds
have returned, circling above.
Are these your fluted wings?

Mountain Cry

You can see the mountain here,
standing on asphalt near
the wheat and the rails, and
from this room eyes closed.
And something else:
the next right idea rising,
a green sun crowning.
Some see it sooner than others—
artists, poets, magicians
with their chalk and string.

Standing with arms raised
to make the north and south of it,
I am a mountain now.
But not for long.
You can see the people
standing in corn, waving
their hair and hunger.
You can see what I mean.
If you let yourself cry for us all
what will it matter
what becomes of the wind?

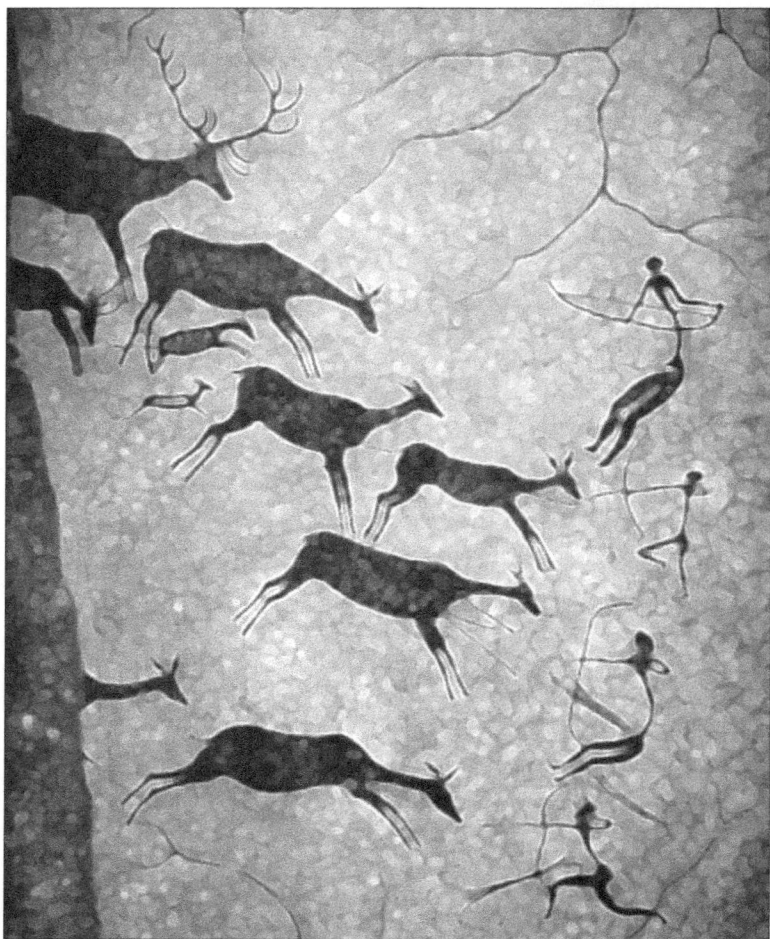

PALMS UP
WITH A BLINDFOLD ON

THE CALL

A wrong number at 9 in the morning:
"Is there a Crystal there?"
"No, there's not," I said.

But there could be. . .

Having just read about retrieving
childhood and the "genius of wonder,"
I was less inclined

to reinforce the world,
the economics of so-called justice,
the crazy way we split it all in two.

I imagined a gazillion crystals,
you can do that as a child,
making up the shape of me,

the diamond of my mind.
All light passes through.

To be *terse* is to be *clear.*
Yes, there is a Crystal here.

Developing Action

We gave the kids throw-away cameras
that they held in front of
tongue-out faces, got-up-late shoes,
stop-to-talk street corners,
brother-mooning butts.

We were summer-lunched;
we were mixed-skin;
we were pre-digital.
We had to wait for development
while bodies grew, shoes
slid on downtown, fathers left
their sleeping-in chairs
for the gone-to-work world.

We got back snap shots
of the already-happened, of the
before-the-haircut head, the
way-it-was-a-week-ago friend.

We found out the past
was a gone-for-good thing.

PUPPET SCRAPS
for Julianna Kirwin

The hawk's shrill cry started to say
that it begins alone and ends there,
but all around no cloud,
nor village, nor wanting mouth
    comes this way
without a pulse.
Deep in the water, down in the rock,
singing in the next cell,
you arrive in every line.

A printmaker ties her apron,
carves flowers behind the ear, begins
in the middle of the moon.
Even her house, tall enough
for the jungle inside, wears the hips
of a hundred women in the walls.

She knows bold dark strokes
but lets the gentle wind in,
    children or orange moths
to light in the trees of her fluid dream.
A hawk high in the ceiling.

To birth a town calls for hands, and
not just two or four.
We'll rename these streets:
"Illumination, Grandbaby Wonder,
Puppet Scraps, Deep Majick."
We'll call the hawk to the table.

THE LISTENING
thinking about Pamela and La Llorona

Every ditch has a cry; every door
bangs like it was the last.
Clouds pass with nothing to say.
Nobody wants to hear your tears.

They keep you busy at stitches,
always at the start of something new.
They string their lights far
into the desert, deep into the hill,
long into the night—blaring—
    a deck of cards stacked
with hairdos, riding machines,
memory in a pinhead.

But night beckons you

to walk alone, to slip into it,
    into the swallowing,
the place they don't dare look.
Crickets sing in summer, then
the slow heaving breath of ice.
These are your friends.

They've known all along
and will not try to fix you, or tell you
what it all means.
Your voice is safe here.

Wail for what you know.

Wail for who you've had to be,
    for who you must become.

The mountain makes the clouds.
Listen—
a trickle of song wets the earth.

HERMIT
for Joe Bottone

In a monastery on the California coast
there's work to do—
the fork and spoon of it,
the mop the floor of it, rocks
to stack after the rain.
There's a lot of time in the chair.

A true hermit does isolation
in broad daylight, averts his eyes,
withholds his touch.
Nothing cast, nothing snagged.
The fog just hangs. Who, then,
is a hermit here?

The road disappears into the sea;
news of war washes up; the gulls
cry as before.
Lipstick stirs
the sacrilege of discontent
and the girls slip by
like slivers of moon
where the city presses hard
against an open heart.

This chamber, or this cell,
those annoyingly slow flies.
Vespers are optional, whispers
to the Virgin private as moss.
Tomorrow, the truck goes to town.

My Brother Still

You would be older now.
You would still be
my brother,
but perhaps cranky
the way a tyrant gets
when their helplessness is obvious
to everyone.

Everything in you would ache
from so much vying
and jostling and deception.
Too much tricky living; more
than just a Scorpio thing.

You might ask for help:
a truck to unload,
an errand to run.
I would be suspicious
of any request, or
any gift for that matter.
I would bring memory to bear
upon the moment—
out of habit.

Out of habit I would see you
as a dark figure
lingering in a doorway.
I would feel tired of withholding.
I would feel guilty.
But why, you used the gun

on yourself, not on me.
Someone should ask:
Where is the love in this?

You wouldn't be that buff young man,
lifting weights and shooting pool,
intimidating me, setting me up
with those zealous detectives
that convicted me at seventeen.
You might be regretful,
or more likely still concerned
with your own betrayal. Whatever—
you would be frail,
the way you always really were.
You would be powerless now
to hurt me.

I took the fall
but it didn't save you, *or them.*
I ate the breadcrumbs
from the breast of our family—
all those imagined sins.

I, who thought I was God,
made darkness my meal,
ate my way toward the light
for us all. I lied.
I didn't let you all the way off the hook.
And, No, you are not older now.

If I made all this up
I would wonder at how I still try
to hold you close, embrace

this wraith of a dream.
I would see my own hand
holding a knife at your back,
at my own back.

I would be the older one now and
since it's clear
that you're not coming back
I might release the hostages.
I might, be your brother after all.

MEN ACROSS THE WATER
for John Roche

Here in the West, we've weathered
our death from Samhain to Ostara—
ice at the edges, cranes
in the wake of light returned,
the close sound of everything stirring.

I read poetry written on a lake
by a man taking refuge
    from sooty bricks
and the stacking of them—
the clack and scrape of eastern institutions.
He, too, is a teacher.

It's good, I say,
to have men in my life.
I know their suffering
    but all too often
have gone only to women for consolation,
and even identity.

We men tinker with things,
not just the wars
with which we're single-handedly credited,
but numerous investigations
of the mind, and of the heart.
    Was it not, after all,
a collusion of the hunt and the hearth?

I've been a man
with rust and mortar on my hands,
the bitter taste of metal.
I've wrecked a lot of cars.
When it's safe, I'll show you
plenty of tears.

On the banks of the Conesus
you set your boat
in the awful knowing of trickery and treaties,
the Iroquois and Seneca still running.
You know sheepberries and northern pike,
    the plight of mallards,
the shrinking of silence.
You remember beaver before the hat.

Brother, I'm half way 'round
this northern turtle, yet I hear
the lapping of water against your boat;
I, too, wrestle with the bear.

TODAY THE PILGRIMS ARRIVED

We heard their stories
and wished them well, well,
not quite so fast. It was the caravan
Libro-traficantes—
Houston, San Antonio, Alburquerque, Tucson.
It was on the road of liberty, it was
on the road of Latin solidarity,
on the road for all the disenfranchised
and trampled and persecuted
in the name of color or tongue
or difference. Difference
without deference. We don't see it
as eating our own.
Only savages are cannibals, after all.

After all the flowers had been thrown,
the speeches, *abrazos*, gas money,
and for God's sake, the books,
the banned books; and after all
the poets had left the hall
    several echoes remained.
I know the names
of heroes whipped to death
in town squares, poisoned
in hospital beds, left to die
in a mountain jungle.
I know an angel when I hear one.

The moment a person calls another "illegal"
they have identified themselves.

This business of identity—how
specialized we have become. These bones
have names; this blood must belong.

We dumped the tea in favor
of a more lucrative party;
we drained the lake
and now we want the water back;
the oppressor and the oppressed dancing
on the dust of all the ideas
of difference that have risen
in our upright posture,
our predator specie, our awkward heart.

Mis Amigos, my many hats are off to you
as you traffic the banned books,
the fanned flame of remembrance.
Travel well, sweet poets,
the border is not the state line.
This is my water; these are my petals
falling before your feet; this
is the lost book of my love.
I have ripped out all the pages but one.

Looking Up from My Shovel

Looking up I wondered if even the worst
of them might be my sisters, my brothers.
Looking up I wondered if they had grain
for breakfast, or food at all.
Looking up from my shovel I crossed the border,
helped them to bury their dead.

In the absence of war we were naked,
our skin clean, beginning to shine.
In the absence of war we were light
on our feet, giddy without metal.
In the absence of war our senses returned.

Return to the fields of sunny corn, return
to the fields of medicine and music.
Return to the table with stories
worthy of telling, stories
of the life you had dared not dream. Return.
Return the birds to light on your hands.

Forward we go with new jobs to do—
what joy to work on a blue green jewel.
Forward we find the map at our feet,
written in the rivers full again.
Forward our thinking reveals intelligence,
balance, reality—love, in other words.

Here the true name of each of us is known.
Here, in the child's hand

is the forgotten stone,
the breath passing between us.

Here are colors never before witnessed,
the friends we couldn't see but knew
must be there, walking with us.
Here, here we are—standing
together in the newly remembered field.

And the Porter Just Smiles

In lines we throw ourselves
across the page, in lines
we draw the curve of you and of me,
     in lines we wait
like empty tables at the station.

Someone has arrived
though their outline is undefined.
She travels light, her story
in the palm of her hand, her history
rolling with the sea.
     Though you offer,
there's nothing to carry.

You speak of her as if love
     were a holy mist, just
a dampness on your hand,
a loveliness even the clouds can't cut.
The wind that sweeps the hills
is no replacement.

Over the speaker another one
     has come and gone.
Between the rails she parts her lips
for the passing of time.
Nothing now but a squeeze in the middle
and the perfume of rain.

OPEN VERSE

When again I looked, I saw
that he was not dying. Old
or young I could not tell,
could no longer speak
for fear's machine, only
this whale-voice-knowing,
this flit-flit bird moment, this
caught in the tumbling light
of perpetual morning.

This time, like no other.

It was not death, not death
as they had said, but a trick
of scarcity and memory,
a sleight of shadow across his face.
He remains. He remains

and we walk
with the original compass,
corn for tooth, blue for yellow,
past the sugar skulls and rattlesnake dances
of false entry and postponement—
each birth bursting forth
from itself, self transcendent.

I am for it—
the wide open spaces
of the poem, the curve
of her that falls forever.

Third Door

Seemed all the coming-going people
had a reason then, a reason
to hold their heads on high,
    or a reason they couldn't.
Seemed there were those of color,
of which I had none.
Seemed there were those
with broken tongues, but I
had silenced myself.

I'll have sirloin, medium rare, blue cheese,
a clean fork if you please.
I'll have an ambulance, some Thorazine,
Alfred Hitchcock in every room.
Seemed my choices were few
in the land of plenty.

I'll have the wolves
beyond the street-lamped town;
    I'll have my voice back
when I find it.

Limp for the god of your choosing, or
kill for the god of your fathers.
No thanks.

Some doors don't know they're closed
until they're opened. Some doors
    aren't doors at all.

Seemed the kings and queens were
cripples then; seemed limping
was its own deadly end.

I'll have my throat back now,
    and whatever lay
behind the *third* door.

There Were Daffodils

> "I left silence, so they could listen to themselves."
> —*It's Raining in Augusta*, Renée Gregorio

Enough of the hollow house
and later episodes of debauchery.
There were daffodils in my mother's garden.

There was Percale, de Haviland, Francis the First,
Tchaikovsky, Robert Lewis Stevenson.
There was a sled with soap for the runners
that belonged to my brother, for nearly
everything came to him first,
but the mittens and forehead kisses
    were my very own.
She tucked me in sober and clean.
She was my mother then.

"When you're halfway up the stairs,
you're half way down."
Mother Goose was lighter than Grimm.
We turned the pages carefully,
magnolias filling summer rooms.

Through open windows, always
a little hammering, some tapping
from a neighbor's shed, a saw
on a bench set in a yard, the yawn of a cat,
the dull ring of stones stacked and fitted.
The noon whistle.

The world was round then: refrigerators,
curve of the hood and trunk, mirror
in the parlor, phonograph records, father's fedora.
Things came around on a regular basis:
bootleggers, Saturday mornings,
valentines, milkmen, tetanus shots.
I'd wake her with a marigold.

I drove the tricycle all by myself.
    I was quiet as a mouse.
I was sitting on the floor humming
in a bar of golden light.
I was recording all this.

Then We're In

I turned through the room
with a stick of white sage,

a river of smoke flowing
from its orange gleed.

Everywhere my hand went
God followed—This, I said,

is to remind me
I need only inquire.

I said, This will remind me
I need only inquire.

Outside the flakes
fell fast, then larger,

then lighter, every which way.
Everywhere: a dream in the air.

I thought of you
in the rain on the coast,

thought of you painting clouds
a thousand miles from water.

I thought of your bodies
being shoveled from streets,

cutting apples for children.
There wasn't anywhere

that didn't have the scent of sage;
then, no more need for hints.

Morning Chores

The coffee maker growls its finish
and you think that's all
poets do: stimulants, ritual, word play.
Today, for reasons
that aren't important now, I thought
about the frontal lobe, that vast continent
of unknown possibilities
with its fledgling coastal towns.
Focus.

I was thinking about focus,
about intent. Stay with me,
not because this is the way, but because
blowing on a coal causes the room
to glow and glow and glow,
and what does it matter
who gets the fire started.
We know those known roads:
you and yours, me and mine,
blah, blah, blah.

It comes down to this—
sloshing in a little boat drifting
into the doldrums of familiar stories
is the surest way to say, I'm offline,
while we let this casing of a mind/body sink
to the dark, silent floor.

I'd rather be surfing!, bent kneed,
fingers tickling the inside wall,

a commuter train screaming through the curl—
evolution. I am the moment
when the wave breaks, roaring
toward the un-invented shore,
scribbling these wet lines
between loads of laundry.

HIDDEN LAKE
for Kathy Park

A week ago I wanted nothing more
than to know the source
of the hidden lake—
the level beneath the level.
Drumming under the moon
and holding my mind just so,
I said I wanted to go there.

Pretty soon everything
was a repeating pattern,
stories forming at the edge.
Any day, I said,
I'd step one degree
to the left and be standing
on the middle of the lake, emptiness
as far as I cared to breath.
I'd know this landscape without a catch.

Since then it snowed; since then
hunger dropped by,
more scratches were found on her
slender marble arms, and the business
of subtraction continued.
The sculptor's obsession.

Standing in a puddle of milky slurry
sanding her muscles to a shine,

I wiped away the waves,
her stone hair and shoulder
appearing above the surface.

It seems this lake comes with a goddess.

IN THE CARDS

I followed the map of mystery
which is no lie, but not
tied to the usual furniture
or choir of neck-tied punksters.
I followed it good

and got lost,
just like I was supposed to,
    like any fool
from a deck of cards would,
like the rain
when you ask it, Which way home?

Eventually, everything crumbles
in your crumbling hand.

After some number of arrests
they said, Stay gone, boy.
That was Oklahoma.
    After that
the streets heaved
but not always psychotropic. Mystery
has no obligation to kindness.
I'm following it now.

I'm hearing the clickity clack of your shoes
on a sidewalk. I'm walking
palms up with a blindfold on.
Sometimes you see me hanging

upside down, but there's a woman
says she sees me
as the Page of Wands.

Afterword

Stewart S. Warren is more than a man. He is a force of nature. He is a conjurer. And he speaks in a conjurer's tongue. When our paths cross, usually at poetry get-togethers, he carries a magic that extends to everyone. He is a rare individual who ignites a secret energy, a primal energy, a luminous force. He is spirit. He is body. He is water. He is fire. He is mystery. And he is everyday life. He is the mystery inherent in everyday life, if one has the eye to recognize it.

I have most recently seen Stewart at gatherings honoring the dead, honoring the recently departed: one honoring poet Todd Moore, the other honoring poet Kell Robertson. Stewart caught the essence of these tributes, for his energy, his spirit carried that which should be carried at such tributes: the ecstatic celebration of rebirth, rejuvenation, transfiguration. Part of the measure of a man is the celebration he inspires after his death, and the transformation of his life into something else. He is here but he is not here. He is not here yet he is here.

My favorite poets are those who carry the overflow of intensified life experience into their poetry. Stewart S. Warren is such a poet. He is Southwest. And he transcends the Southwest. He is one with the landscape. And his language is electric, with an amazing sense of time, of place, of space. In the poem "Day After the Rain" it is not the visceral experience of the day of the rain, but the day after, life resumed after the storm. It is the cyclical nature, the evolution and revolution, of the universe.

And then there are those poems which reveal all levels of reality at once. "Ice Ball Returning" is such a poem. Poems in which every word contributes to a whole that is as elusive as it is real. Poems in which the conjure is so strong that you can feel the magic working in every line. "Ice Ball Returning" does just that with unforgettable lines such as "I didn't so much mind the dust/and the lopsided shingle/but doubting the dream was certain hell." Lines like "I've been late for class, late for dinner/ and late for death;/I've been slow to pull and slow/to get the essence of her complaints./It's a fact: I just don't straighten up good." And there is the ending of the poem that is simply breathtaking, following "the appetite of a far flung comet/entering the orbit of true outlaws."

Stewart S. Warren brings the magic, brings the marvelous, brings the mojo. His writings, his performances, his appearances yield a Southwest magus suffused with his own brand of poetry. In this book, his amazing poetry is contrasted with some startlingly beautiful images. The combination is mesmerizing. The messages are exhilarating. He reveals that it is "enough to be earth." He reads poetry "written on a lake." He speaks of "the beauty that sets fire to the wind." And, most of all, he announces a rare brotherhood in which "we go up in the same flame." As he says, "Longing is a flame/I keep in my window. This burning/of borders, this fire between us./There's room for you here. Here/there is also burning."

Tony A. Moffeit
Author of *Poetry is Dangerous, the Poet is an Outlaw*
and *Born to Be Blue*

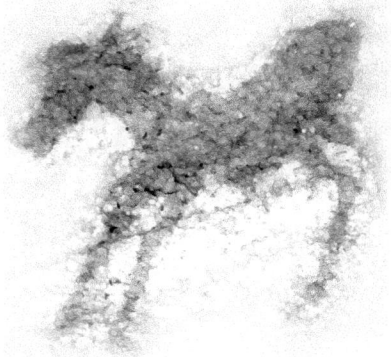

ALBUQUERQUE, NEW MEXICO 2012

About the Author

Born and partly raised in eastern Oklahoma, at the age of seventeen Stewart Warren became a convicted felon. He holds no university degrees. Neither of these details have hindered his passions nor his abilities to be a writer and a teacher. Quite the contrary.

Earlier in his life Stewart travelled throughout North America, catching rides at truck stops, small plane terminals and along farm to market roads while working his way through a variety of cultures and landscapes from Haight Ashbury to Cuernavaca. In more recent decades he has settled into a pattern of small migrations through southern Colorado and northern New Mexico, following an "unseen friend" on a path of self discovery and camaraderie with fellow travellers.

As a publishing coach and an organizer of community events, Stewart assists others in deepening their creative experience and realizing their artistic visions.

www.ingramcontent.com/pod-product-compliance
Lightning Source LLC
Chambersburg PA
CBHW051827040426
42447CB00006B/398